Curious COACHING QUESTIONS

Mini Pocket Guide for Expanding Awareness

Pamela Richarde

CONTENTS

INTRODUCTION

As humans, communication is fundamental to our nature. From our earliest days, we learn to speak and engage with the world through curiosity. Yet as we grow, the instinct to wonder can quiet, the habit of questioning often fades, and our natural inquisitiveness may be overshadowed by certainty, speed, or self-protection. This guide is here to help rekindle that innate curiosity, both as a way of being and as a core coaching skill, inviting us back into the art of exploration.

In coaching and other helping professions, we are always deepening our ability to communicate, both with others and with ourselves. At the heart of this work is curiosity: the willingness to witness, inquire, and not know. Our profession rests on a foundation of presence: we listen, we ask, we reflect, we clarify. We hold space for insight to arise and for transformation to unfold. And while our work is grounded in rigor and intention, it is also a practice of wonder. It is both skillful and sacred.

This guide focuses on one of the most powerful tools in communication: the question. Specifically, how we can use thoughtful, curious questions to uncover insight, challenge assumptions, illuminate new paths, and spark self-awareness.

Our aim here is not to "train" you in the art of questioning. Rather, this resource is offered in the spirit of practice, reflection, and creative expansion. Skill development is an ongoing path, and we all benefit from new language, fresh prompts, and unexpected doorways along the way. We've created this collection of questions to inspire you, stir your thinking, and expand the edges of your own voice.

These questions are simply starting points, organized by topic but not confined to one context. They are meant to be adapted and shaped to fit your style. Use them as springboards for deeper presence. Let them evolve into your own authentic expressions. And most importantly, ask them from a place of not-knowing.

Asking with a predetermined answer in mind can close the space for discovery. But asking with curiosity, without attachment, opens a field of possibility. This is where insight lives. This is where the person being questioned can find what is true for them. Stay open. Let go of needing to be right. Let the questions do their quiet work.

QUESTIONS:
More Than We Realize

We use questions constantly, sometimes consciously, often reflexively. But how often do we pause to consider what they truly are, or the ripple they can create in another? Let's take a breath together here and expand our understanding of questions beyond their common use as tools for extracting information.

The Oxford English Dictionary defines the verb to question as: "The action of inquiry or asking. The stating or investigation of a problem: inquiry into a matter."

It's a solid place to begin. But questions are much more than this. They are educators, catalysts, connectors, and sometimes even disruptors. They can open doors or close them, illuminate or obscure. Questions are powerful and capable of sparking curiosity, provoking insight, deepening understanding and inviting transformation. They can be tools or torches that illuminate bridges, maps, mirrors or even boundaries.

Exploring the nature of questions is an enriching, often surprising path. The more deeply we reflect on the role questions play, the more we see how they shape our relationships, our self-awareness, and the way we navigate the world. While a full exploration is beyond the scope of this booklet, we offer this working definition, rooted in a coaching lens: A question is the seeking of information for clarity, insight, and learning.

This simple framing invites us to ask not just for answers but for expansion. To listen with openness. To ask with presence. To honor the unknown.

Whether you are a coach, entrepreneur, executive, parent, therapist, artist, teacher or simply a human walking through life, we hope the questions and reflections offered here will support you in communicating with more clarity, curiosity, and grace. Because sometimes, one truly curious question can shift everything.

IMPACT

Most of our interactions, whether personal, professional, or somewhere in between, rely deeply on how we communicate. And at the heart of that communication live questions: ever-present, often overlooked, and always impactful.

As Dr. Marilee Goldberg writes in The Art of the Question (1998), "Despite the omnipresence of questions in our lives, few people are fully aware of the potential and power inherent in them."

Indeed, questions are more than tools. They are touchstones of relationship, and they reveal, reframe, reflect and open minds or shut them. They can gently guide or subtly manipulate, build bridges or trigger barriers.

The impact of a question lies not only in what is asked, but how it is asked: with openness or agenda, with presence or distraction, with curiosity or conclusion. A powerful question does not force movement; it invites emergence. It doesn't insist on an answer; it makes space for discovery. When delivered with attunement, free of judgment or attachment to outcome, a question becomes a catalyst. It offers a moment of pause, a flicker of possibility, a path toward deeper clarity. Whether you are coaching a client, mentoring a colleague, leading a team, or having tea with a friend, the quality of your questions matters.

In our work as coaches, we've learned this truth repeatedly: it's not that people don't have answers, it's that they haven't yet been asked the question that unlocks the door. Or the question hasn't yet arrived with the spaciousness, kindness, or equanimity needed to be received.

A truly skillful question is a quiet revolution. It can shift a narrative, illuminate a belief, soften a defense, or awaken a dormant dream. And its impact, when asked from a place of deep presence, can be profound.

WAY OF BEING

The art of questioning has many layers. Some are seen. Some are felt. Over time, through experience, reflection, and presence, we learn to trust the process of asking questions not just as a technique, but as an extension of who we are.

There are many types of questions, and many ways to ask them. But rarely is it about "getting it right." What matters just as much as what we ask is how, why, and from where the question is asked. In other words, what is the way of being behind the question?

In coaching, this becomes essential. A question asked out of judgment will land differently from one asked from curiosity. A question asked to shift the client's energy will feel different than one asked to prove a point. That's why it's helpful to ask not just, "What question should I ask?" but also, "Who is this question for?"and "What part of me is asking it?"

Let's consider a simple, everyday example: You notice the kitchen trash is full. It's your youngest daughter's responsibility, and she hasn't taken it out. From the bottom of the stairs, you call up: "Antoinette, have you taken out the trash?" Of course, you already know the answer. So why pose it as a question? Is your intent to educate? To remind? To subtly reprimand? Your tone and your energy will carry your message before your words even land.

If your intention is simply to remind her, your voice might be neutral, easygoing. The question may prompt a quick, "Oops! I'll get it." But if this has become a recurring issue, your tone might tighten, your patience fray, and now the question carries a veiled charge. Tension enters the room, even before she does. This is the subtle and powerful dance of presence. It's not just what we ask, but how we ask it. And why.

Mastering the art of questioning invites us to turn inward, to reflect on our own way of being, our patterns of thought, and our deeper intentions. As our self-awareness grows, so too does the quality of our questions. Our presence becomes the container. Our curiosity becomes the invitation. And over time, with practice, we begin to find the right questions, not from technique or effort, but from attunement and alignment.

As you move through this booklet, we offer this as a compass. A soft reminder to listen inward as you speak outward. To notice not only what you ask, but who you are in the asking. And one day, we imagine this guide will sit quietly on the shelf because you'll be living the questions, moment by moment, with presence, compassion, and clarity.

CURIOSITY:
The Art and Practice of Wondering

Before we dive into the questions that follow, it's essential to pause and reflect on something foundational: curiosity. It is the heartbeat of every great question, the doorway to insight, and the thread that ties listening to discovery.

As mentioned earlier, mastery in the art of asking powerful questions, whether for yourself or others, begins with deep, attuned listening. From that still place, we cultivate genuine curiosity about what we're hearing, sensing, knowing and just as importantly, what we don't yet know. When we approach life and conversation with true curiosity, we open the space for transformation to emerge.

It is not just the techniques we learn that shape our effectiveness, but who we are being while using them. Knowing how to ask a question is one thing. But the energy we bring to that moment, our presence, intention, and attitude, makes all the difference. This brings us to a guiding truth:

Curiosity isn't a strategy; it's a way of being.

When we meet others with wholehearted curiosity, we create safety. We signal openness. We invite co-discovery. We plant the seeds for learning, connection, and meaningful change.

Building the Curiosity Muscle

So how do we strengthen our ability to be curious, especially in a world that so often demands certainty and answers?

Psychologist Mihaly Csikszentmihalyi, in his work "Flow", noted that we can develop our curiosity and disrupt boredom by intentionally directing our attention toward something specific in our environment. The simple act of focusing deeply becomes a portal for wonder.

As coaches, leaders, and communicators, this translates into becoming curious explorers of the human experience, turning toward our clients, our conversations, our relationships, and even ourselves, with fresh eyes and open hearts.

Curiosity can be strengthened like any muscle. The more you stretch it, play with it, and trust it, the more it grows.

Tips for Cultivating Curiosity

- Be a learner. Be curious not only about what you don't know, but even more about what you think you do know.

- Be comfortable saying "I don't know". Resting in not-knowing can be a rich soil for discovery.

- Seek out other perspectives. Remember: your way of seeing isn't the only way. Explore how others view the world.

- Model and reward curiosity. Your own wonderment can inspire those around you to open and explore.

- Ask first, before telling. Questions invite expansion; advice can sometimes limit the field.

- Try new things. Engage with unfamiliar experiences to loosen the grip of certainty.

- Pause. Notice. Play. Stop. Look. Listen. Let yourself have fun in the process.

Curiosity is a key, one that unlocks the inherent wisdom within every human being. It nurtures inquiry, self-reflection, creativity, and possibility. It is the light we shine into the corners of the unknown, the food we offer to the seeds of greatness waiting quietly in the soil of our inner life.

So, remember what it felt like to be as curious as a young child. Practice bringing that energy into all that you do. Make curiosity your companion. And, as always, let it be joyful.

TOOLS FOR BUILDING

The primary tools for cultivating curiosity are, of course, questions. But questions are more than tools. They are steppingstones, lanterns, and gentle chisels we use to sculpt insight, open doors, and build bridges between where we are and where we're going.

This guide offers a curated collection, a kind of mini library of curious inquiry, organized around different domains of human experience. Each section begins with a brief reflection to lay the ground, followed by questions you can draw from, adapt, or simply let inspire you.

You might find one question is enough to open a whole world. Or that a cluster of them lights up a new direction. Some questions will feel energizing, others gently confronting. All of them are invitations.

There's no particular order to how you use this resource. One playful way to explore it is to open the pages at random when you're feeling stuck or seeking direction. Trust that the question that finds you might be just the one that's needed in that moment.

You don't need to memorize these questions or get them "right." Let them be like tools in a beloved, well-used toolbox, ready when called, flexible in their purpose, and shaped by your own voice.

Use this booklet to stir your own curiosity. Practice asking from presence, listening from openness, and trusting the emergent path. With time, you may find that the best questions are the ones you didn't expect to ask. Above all, enjoy your exploration and follow your wonder. Let your questions be the compass that guides you deeper into knowing and not-knowing, and the beautiful terrain in between.

WHAT GIFTS ARE READY TO BE REMEMBERED?

Everyone carries unique gifts, innate ways of seeing, being, creating, and connecting that are theirs alone to express. Yet often, these gifts lie hidden beneath layers of doubt, conditioning, or simply the distractions of daily life. Some people may not yet recognize the brilliance they carry; others may have glimpsed it but hesitate to claim it fully, unsure of how it will be received or whether it truly "counts."

And yet our gifts are not meant to be hoarded or perfected before being shared. They are meant to be lived into, remembered, and offered. When we as coaches, friends, or fellow travelers gently invite someone to notice, explore, and own their gifts, we become mirrors for what is already true. We help rekindle a sacred remembering.

In this space of curiosity and compassion, we open the possibility for others to rediscover their strengths, not as something to fix or improve, but as something to honor and embody. This remembering becomes a powerful foundation for growth, courage, and meaningful contribution.

The questions that follow are offered to invite reflection and spark the quiet remembering of one's gifts, of who they are, and perhaps, who they may have forgotten they've always been.

- What comes naturally to you?

- What gifts do you believe you were born with?

- Are the gifts others see in you different from the ones you recognize in yourself?

- What activities fill you with joy?

- In how many ways do you express your creativity?

- What might you shift or release in to fully embody your gift?

- What are you truly meant to be doing?

- What is worth building your life around?

- What feels like it's holding you back from pursuing what you love?

SUPPORTIVE RESOURCES, RESERVES AND WHAT YOU DESERVE

Support in life takes many forms, some visible and tangible, others quiet and subtle. One key to navigating life with resilience and grace is learning to recognize what supports you, where that support comes from, and how much of it you have access to in any given moment.

This is about more than just resources. It's about knowing how to tap into what's available, your inner capacities, relationships, environment, intuition and how to replenish them when needed. It's also about understanding your reserves, those extra stores of energy, time, connection, or clarity that sustain you when the road is long. Like a bit of fuel hidden in the tank, reserves don't need to be drawn on all the time, but knowing they're there, brings ease and strength.

And underlying it all is this vital question: Do you believe you deserve support?

Because if you don't believe you're worthy of being resourced, nourished, and held, you may not even notice the possibilities that surround you.

When you honor your worth, your eyes begin to open. You start to recognize the wellsprings within and around you and from that place, you're able to receive, replenish, and extend your impact in the world.

The questions below invite you to explore your landscape of support, resources, reserves, and your sense of what you truly deserve.

- What support do you currently have in place?

- What resources do you need to create what you want?

- How can you make the most of the resources you already have?

- What kind of support will help move things forward?

- Who are your biggest advocates and supporters?

- How much is enough? (In terms of time, space, love, money, etc.)

- What might happen if you simply asked for what you need?

- What is holding you back from creating what you deserve?

- What limiting beliefs might be shaping your sense of deserving?

- What will it take for you to have everything you need, want, and desire?

WANTS, NEEDS & THE WISDOM TO KNOW THE DIFFERENCE

Understanding the difference between what you want and what you need can bring profound clarity. It helps untangle the threads of desire, survival, fulfillment, and choice making it easier to recognize what truly matters.

Wants are often desirable, motivating, and even joyful like a beautiful home, a luxurious vacation, or an inspired creative project. These desires can reflect your values, your aesthetic, and your longings for expansion. Sometimes though, what appears to be a want may be a deeper need in disguise. A promotion, a romantic ideal, or even a creative ambition might seem like external goals, when underneath, there's a longing for acknowledgment, safety, or belonging. While they can inspire movement forward, they are not always essential for your immediate well-being.

Needs, on the other hand, are the foundational elements that allow you to feel whole and safe. Things like love, belonging, nourishment, rest, and emotional acknowledgment. When our core needs go unmet, they can quietly (or loudly) shape our decisions and behaviors, often without our full awareness.

Becoming conscious of the distinction between what you want and what you need doesn't diminish the value of either. In fact, it creates a kind of inner alignment, so that your choices are guided not by unconscious urgency, but by clarity, wholeness, and self-honoring.

The questions below are here to support that exploration.

- What is the difference between what you want and what you need in this moment of your life?

- How can you tell if an unmet need is quietly influencing your choices?

- How do you know that what you think you want is truly what you desire?

- What are you attached to in this pursuit and what might be underneath that attachment?

- What will having this truly give you?

- If your house were on fire, what would you carry out with you?

- What is driving this goal: fear, hope, longing, love or something else?

- How much is this costing you emotionally, energetically, or otherwise?

- What would be different if you truly believed you are already enough?

- What if you already have what you truly need?

THE LENS OF TRUTH:
What Filters Your Reality?

At the core of our integrity as human beings is the ability to discern and live in alignment with our truth. But truth is rarely simple. It is personal, evolving, and often buried beneath layers of habit, protection, or expectation. Your truth may not match someone else's, and that's not a flaw, it's a reflection of the unique perspective each of us brings to life.

Choosing to speak your truth or to avoid it, has a profound impact on your energy, your relationships, and your sense of wholeness. Avoiding or suppressing what feels true for you isn't merely a distraction; it creates inner tension, dissonance, and often a slow drain on your vitality. Sometimes, your truth isn't hidden, it's just hard to say out loud. And other times, it has become obscured by small, daily compromises made to feel safe, accepted, or in control.

To live in alignment with your truth means to first be honest with yourself:

- What am I pretending not to know?

- Where am I out of alignment with what I say I value?

- What truth, if spoken, would set me free?

- Truth is not a weapon. It is a clearing. It doesn't have to be loud to be powerful. It just must be real.

The questions that follow are here to help you explore your relationship with truth—your truth, and the truths that shape how you move through the world.

- What is important to you about telling the truth?

- If there were no consequences, what would feel most true for you in this situation?

- When do you tend to avoid sharing your truth and why?

- What's feels at risk for you in being fully honest here?

- What happens in your body when you don't speak your truth?

- Whose truth is this, yours, or someone else's that you've taken on?

- What do you really believe about this situation?

- What else might also be true?

- How might your life shift if you truly began living from your own truth?

- How can you be just a little more authentically you today?

BECOMING: WHAT'S EMERGING NOW?

Life is a constant unfolding, an ever-shifting dance of movement, growth, stillness, and change. Much like the turning of the seasons, our personal journeys are marked by cycles of blossoming and letting go, of expansion and retreat. Some moments feel like summer: bright, easeful, and full of bloom. Others feel more like winter: quiet, uncertain, even barren. Yet in every season, something essential is being cultivated.

To move forward doesn't always mean to move fast. Sometimes it means pausing, rooting more deeply, or choosing a new direction with greater clarity.

Understanding what nourishes your growth in each unique phase of life, what "fertilizer" supports you in the different "soils" of your experience, can help you navigate transitions with more ease and compassion. Whether you're emerging from challenge, standing at a threshold, or preparing to leap into something new, your inner wisdom can guide the way.

The questions that follow are offered to help you reflect, realign, and choose your next step with presence and intention.

- What does "moving forward" look or feel like for you right now?

- What belief might need to shift for you to take your next step?

- Are you living your life or someone else's version of it?

- What's one thing you could simplify that would create more space for growth?

- What will support you in taking the next step?

- What are you willing to do and by when?

- What are two actions you can take right now to move forward?

- What might be possible if you chose success?

- What could prevent you from moving forward

- How might you meet that challenge with compassion?

- How will you recognize your progress along the way?

- What's beyond this current challenge or obstacle?

- What are you building, not just achieving?

VALUES: WHAT TRULY MATTERS TO YOU?

Living a life rooted in what truly matters is one of the surest ways to feel whole, present, and fulfilled. When you're grounded in your core values, those quiet, powerful truths that shape your sense of rightness and resonance, both the joys and the challenges of life become easier to navigate. Decisions gain clarity and boundaries become clearer. Life begins to feel more aligned, even when it's complex.

Your values are like the hearth at the center of your being quiet, steady, and essential. They warm your choices, illuminate your direction, and offer a deep sense of belonging when the world around you feels chaotic or uncertain. When you live in alignment with these inner flames, life becomes not just manageable, but meaningful.

And yet, many people feel disconnected from what truly matters to them. Over time, the noise of the world expectations, obligations, routines, and distractions can pull us away from our deeper knowing. We forget. We compromise. We adapt so much that our true values become blurred.

Reconnecting with your values is not about getting the "right" answer. It's about remembering. Remembering what moved you when you were younger. Remembering what fills you with meaning now. Remembering what you want your life to stand for.

Your values are also like a garden living, evolving, and asking for your attention. Some values may remain constant, while others shift with the seasons of your life. When you take the time to notice what's growing well, what needs pruning, and what needs replanting, you begin to consciously cultivate a life that reflects who you truly are.

These values, your hearth and your garden, form the inner architecture of a life that is not just productive, but deeply lived.

The questions that follow are here to help you reconnect with what matters most—to you.

- What personal guiding principles shape how you live, work, and love?

- What is most important to you in life right now, in this season?

- What did you want to be or do when you were younger?

- What activities make you lose track of time and feel most alive?

- What do you value most in your current relationships?

- What is the gap between what you love and what you are currently doing?

- How does this (decision/situation/relationship) fit into the bigger picture of your life?

- Which of your values is this choice or challenge bumping up against?

- What matters about your ideal outcome?

- What might you need to shift to bring this more into alignment with what you believe?

- When everything else is stripped away, how does this resonate with you?

- What do you want to be remembered for?

HOW DO YOU TEND TO YOUR OWN WHOLENESS?

As we grow, much of what we learn is centered on how to care for others, how to show up, be responsible, meet expectations, and do the right thing. And while we may be taught the basics of personal upkeep; brushing our teeth, eating well, staying clean, doing our homework, we are often not taught how to truly care for ourselves in ways that nourish the soul.

Self-care is not just about maintenance; it is about presence. It's about remembering that you are not just a vessel for doing, but a being who is worthy of tending.

True self-care goes beyond the basics. It includes honoring your rhythms. It means pausing when you're weary, playing when you've forgotten how, stretching when you've grown still, and returning to joy when life feels too heavy. It's found in moments of creative flow, spontaneous laughter, quiet solitude, gentle movement, honest boundaries, and intentional replenishment. It is the practice of listening inward and responding with kindness not just occasionally, but regularly, as an act of sacred partnership with yourself.

Tending to yourself is not selfish. It is how you stay resourced enough to offer your best self to the world without losing her in the process.

The questions below are here to support your reflection on what self-care means to you, and how it might become a deeper part of your daily life.

- How well are you taking care of yourself in body, mind, heart, and spirit?

- What does rest and replenishment look like for you?

- What would it feel like to take extraordinary care of yourself?

- When was the last time you did something just because?

- What really makes you laugh, belly and all?

- What are your health and well-being goals?

- What distractions keep you from fully relaxing or being present?

- When is it okay for you to be just as important as everyone else?

- What would it look like if you just took a day to yourself?

- What message might your body or the universe be trying to send you?

- What lesson do you keep encountering again and again about how you treat yourself?

- Will you stop and listen to yourself today?

SAYING NO TO SAY YES

"NO" is a complete sentence. Full stop. End of story. And yet, is that true for you?

For many of us, especially in roles as coaches, caregivers, leaders, colleagues, or family members, saying "no" is one of the hardest things to do. And when we finally do say it, we often feel compelled to defend, explain, and justify ("dexify") to soften the blow. We offer reasons, justifications, or long-winded apologies to ease our own discomfort or someone else's disappointment.

But saying "no" isn't unkind. In fact, it can be one of the most loving things you do for yourself and for others.

Your ability to say "no" is deeply connected to the boundaries and inner standards you hold. It reflects how clearly you know your values, how much you honor your time and energy, and how willing you are to protect what matters most.

Think of saying "no" as closing the gate to your inner garden. Not to keep people out, but to ensure what's growing within you has space to thrive. Or like the tide pulling back, so the shore can breathe and reset. When you say "no" to what isn't aligned, you create room to say a wholehearted "yes" to what is.

Learning to say "no" with clarity and grace doesn't mean being rigid or harsh. It means being in integrity with your energy, your truth, and your priorities.

The questions below are here to help you explore your relationship with "no" and what "yes" it might be making room for.

- How comfortable are you with saying "no" to others?

- What has kept you from saying "no" in the past?

- What need might be driving you to say "yes" by default?

- What is your personal filter for making decisions?

- How does saying "yes" to this align or misalign with your current priorities?

- When you say "yes" to that, what are you saying "no" to?

- What support would help you say "no" more confidently and clearly?

- What will saying "no" give you that you haven't had before?

- What would it feel like to say "no" with kindness and a smile?

- What do you need to say "no" to just for today?

- What would change if you began to treat "no" as a complete sentence?

- What will you be able to say a truer yes to when you honor your no?

WHERE IS YOUR ENERGY GOING?

We don't always realize how much energy we're leaking.

We move through the day doing responding, reacting, checking off tasks without always noticing where our time, attention, and vitality are quietly being spent. But just like a bucket with a slow, steady leak, even the smallest cracks in awareness can leave us feeling depleted.

In coaching, we often name these hidden energy drains as "tolerations." Tolerations are the things you put up with, the small annoyances, unspoken resentments, unresolved tasks, or recurring frustrations that take up space in your inner landscape. They may not seem significant on their own, but over time, they pull on your attention like invisible threads, leaving you tired, distracted, or disoriented.

Energy drains can show up in any area of life: your environment, your relationships, your habits, your schedule, even your inner dialogue. And here's the powerful part: once you name them, you begin to reclaim your energy. Awareness is the first step to renewal.

Think of it like patching the leaks in your energetic vessel so your life force can be used more intentionally, more joyfully, and more fully in alignment with what truly matters.

The questions that follow are here to help you identify where your energy may be leaking and how you might begin to call it back.

- What is putting up with that costing you?

- What situation feels unresolved, and how long have you been carrying it?

- What makes you feel tired just thinking about it?

- Do you wake up with a full tank or already running low?

- What consumes most of your time, attention, or emotional bandwidth?

- What support do you need to begin recharging your internal batteries?

- What boundary could you set to create more space and energy for yourself?

- What personal standard might you raise to reclaim more of your power?

- What would shift if you simply stopped putting up with this?

- What is your biggest energy drain right now?

- What two things are you willing to stop tolerating this month?

- What will you gain, emotionally, mentally, or physically, by letting go of this drain?

LIT FROM WITHIN: What Sparks Your Fire?

Without the spark of passion, life can begin to feel flat, like living in black and white. Passion brings color. It brings vitality. It animates our days with meaning and aliveness. And yet, many people find themselves disconnected from their passions. For some, passion feels like a memory from a former version of themselves. For others, it feels buried under layers of responsibility, fatigue, or the subtle weight of "shoulds." You may not even realize how far away you've drifted from what once lit you up.

But here's the truth: Passion doesn't disappear. It waits. It simmers beneath the surface, patiently longing to be rekindled. Passion isn't always loud or grand. Sometimes it's quiet. A curiosity, a creative spark, a longing to explore, to express, to move, to build, to serve, to play. It doesn't have to be career-defining or world-changing. It only must be true to you.

Reconnecting with your passion is not just about feeling more excitement. It's about reclaiming a vital part of yourself. Passion energizes. It brings clarity. It reignites interest in your work, your relationships, and your daily rhythm. It makes waking up feel like a welcome beginning, not just another obligation. Think of your passion as a hidden ember, waiting to be fanned back to life. Or as a compass made of longing, pointing toward what matters most.

The questions below are here to help you explore, rediscover, and honor the passions that live within you, whether they are roaring flames or quiet whispers waiting to be heard.

- What brings a smile to your face when you think about it every time?

- What do you just love, love, LOVE doing?

- When does time seem to disappear for you?

- What activities naturally energize or uplift you?

- What sparks your creativity or your desire to create?

- When you're being creative, what fuels your passion in the process?

- What does passion bring to your life emotionally, spiritually, practically?

- If you could design your life around what you love, what would it look and feel like?

- What changes might help you bring more passion back into your daily life?

- What's standing in the way of expressing your passion more freely?

- Whose voice is getting in the way of your joy?

- What's one small step you could take to fan the flames of your passion today?

WHAT WILL MAKE THE DIFFERENCE?

Sometimes, it's not about doing more. It's about doing one thing differently.

Perhaps a shift in focus, a new question, a boundary spoken aloud, a weekend of rest or simply a single moment of courage.

There are times in life when a small, thoughtful change becomes the hinge that opens a heavy door. When we pause and ask, *what will make the difference here?* we begin to look not for more effort, but for more alignment.

In coaching, this is often where the breakthrough begins. Even asking the "wrong" question can reveal the path by showing us what doesn't matter. And the "right" question? It can create a ripple that alters the entire course of a conversation, a decision, even a life. Think of this moment like a fulcrum point, the place where the right amount of intention, placed in the right direction, can move the seemingly unmovable. Or like a key, simple in shape, but essential in unlocking the next room of possibility.

The questions that follow are here to help you explore that leverage point, that breath of insight. That small shift that might change everything.

- What is the one small thing that would make the biggest difference in your life right now?

- What's standing in your way?

- If one resource could change everything, what would it be?

- What attitude shift might change how you meet this moment?

- What can you let go of that you wouldn't even miss?

- What will make this project or this season feel easier, more aligned, or more alive?

- What are you already doing that's contributing to your progress?

- What if your current perspective is only one small window in a larger house?

- Who in your life consistently makes a meaningful difference?

- What would change if you trusted that the difference is already unfolding?

THE DANCE OF ENOUGH

For many of us, life can feel like a constant race, with so many roles, so many responsibilities, all asking for our time, energy, and attention. We move fast, often without pause, and before long we forget what it feels like to breathe deeply, rest fully, or choose our pace.

When we're out of balance, life can begin to feel fragmented like we're chasing something just out of reach. There never seems to be quite enough: enough time, enough rest, enough money, enough meaning, enough US.

But balance isn't a fixed point or a perfect split between work and play, doing and being. Balance is personal. It's a rhythm, a conversation between your inner world and your outer reality. What feels balanced for one person may feel constricting or chaotic for another.

Think of balance like a tree in the wind, rooted, but flexible. Or like a dancer, shifting weight moment by moment to remain centered in motion.

It's not about achieving stillness, it's about discovering what steadies you, what nourishes you, what allows you to show up fully without losing yourself in the swirl.

The questions below are here to help you reflect on what balance means for you, not as an ideal, but as a lived, breathing state of being.

- Where in your life do you feel most out of balance, and how does it show up?

- What are you leaving out of your life that you quietly miss?

- What feels overwhelming or "too much" right now?

- What are the warning signs that you've reached your limit?

- What does it cost you emotionally, physically, or spiritually—when you don't listen to your body's needs?

- How do you feel when you actually have time to rest or recharge?

- What are you sacrificing to keep everything going?

- If your life felt more balanced, what would that look and feel like for you?

- What would you like more time or space for?

- Where is the one place you feel most centered and at peace?

- What's the missing piece in your life's puzzle and how might you gently welcome it in?

- If you could do one small thing this week to restore balance, what would it be?

BECOMING WHAT'S NEXT

Change is woven into the fabric of life. Like the seasons, it comes whether we're ready or not sometimes gentle, sometimes sudden, sometimes long-awaited. It's part of every growth cycle, every relationship, every breath of becoming.

And yet many of us resist it. Even when we long for something new, we often cling to the familiar. Not because we don't want change but because change asks us to loosen our grip, to surrender certainty, to let go of who we were to make space for who we're becoming.

Change is rarely comfortable. But it can be sacred.

How we relate to change shapes our journey through it. When we resist, we often feel friction, confusion, or overwhelm. But when we meet change with curiosity, even cautious curiosity, we begin to move with it rather than against it. In this space, even the messiness of transition can become a place of creative possibility.

Think of change like a river reshaping its course, carving away what no longer serves, revealing new edges, and inviting fresh landscapes into view. Or like the turning of a season, inevitable, natural, and full of subtle wisdom.

The questions below are here to help you explore your relationship with change. To notice what you're resisting, what you're ready for, and what life might be trying to invite you into next.

- What changes are unfolding in your life right now inside or out?

- What change are you quietly longing for?

- What feels most uncomfortable about this change?

- What is this discomfort pointing to?

- Where in your body do you feel resistance to this change?

- What's the story you're telling yourself about this change?

- What would help you feel more supported or grounded during this transition?

- What are the gifts or possibilities hidden within this change?

- What if nothing changed, how would that feel one year from now?

- How have you already changed in ways you didn't expect?

- What does the "next level" of your life or work look like on the other side of this?

- What's one thing you could shift today to begin moving with this change, not against it?

- What new order might be waiting just beyond this moment of chaos?

WHAT DOES YOUR LIFE LOOK LIKE?

In the fullness of daily living, it's easy to stay busy, checking boxes, moving forward, doing what needs to be done. But without moments of pause, we may suddenly realize that the life we're living no longer feels like it belongs to us. Just as an artist steps back to see the whole canvas, we too must step back from time to time to notice what's taking shape. To ask: Is this the life I meant to create? Does it reflect who I'm becoming?

We are each both the artist and the artwork. Every choice, every season, every no and yes, every dream delayed or followed are brushstrokes. Textures. Color. Space. If we don't take the time to check in, we might find that what we're painting no longer reflects our inner vision. But when we do pause, we can revise. We can reimagine. We can begin again—not from scratch, but from truth. Your life is not a product to perfect; it's a process to live into. A story to tell. A picture that evolves with you.

The questions that follow are here to help you step back from the canvas and look with loving, honest eyes at the life you are shaping and the future it's quietly calling forth.

- How do you define success for you, not for anyone else?

- What does your life feel like right now; a smile, a sigh, a sprint or something else?

- What are you most proud of in your life so far?

- What part of your life is unfolding with joy and what part feels left behind?

- Where are you in the process of creating the life you want?

- What are you doing right now to nourish a dream that matters to you?

- How are you making space for creativity, laughter, or play in your daily life?

- What are you resisting, and how might that resistance be protecting you?

- Where are you placing your attention?

- What would it take for you to feel whole and complete in this season of life?

- What outcome are you quietly hoping for?

- What's one step you could take toward what you want to create?

- What might your life look like if it truly reflected the truth of who you are becoming?

BRIDGING THE SPACE BETWEEN

Communication is more than words; it's the invisible thread that connects us to one another. Every sigh, every silence, every gesture, every question, it all speaks. And yet, for something so essential to human connection, many of us were never taught how to communicate with clarity, presence, and compassion. We picked up patterns from our families, our culture, our wounds. We learned how to speak, perhaps but not always how to listen. Or how to truly feel heard.

Right now, in this very moment, you are communicating. By reading this. By reflecting. By how your body is responding to this page; your breath, your posture, even your quiet "mmm."

Strong communication lives at the intersection of expression and reception how we share what's inside us, and how we meet what's inside others. When we become more intentional with how we communicate, we strengthen not just our relationships, but our leadership, our presence, our ability to create impact.

So what makes communication clear? Authenticity. Curiosity. The willingness to ask questions not just to be right, but to understand. Think of communication as a bridge built moment by moment, word by word. Or as water able to flow, to ripple, to carry meaning across distance and difference. And like any skill, it deepens with awareness, reflection, and feedback.

The questions that follow are here to help you listen more deeply to your own voice, and to the voices around you.

- What does it feel like when someone gives you their full attention?

- How well do you truly listen not just to words, but to what's beneath them?

- How often are you waiting for your chance to speak, rather than listening to understand?

- What are you usually focused on while someone else is speaking?

- What makes you want to listen deeply to someone?

- How do you show someone, verbally or nonverbally, that you truly heard them?

- What is your natural speaking pace fast and flowing, or slow and spacious?

- When you're unsure about something, how does that affect your communication style?

- What have others said about your ability to listen or to get your point across?

- How do others respond when you speak a strong truth?

- When have you sensed something unspoken in a conversation?

- What would it feel like to allow more silence to exist between your questions?

WHEN INSIGHT BECOMES MOVEMENT

All the dreaming, reflecting, planning, and visioning in the world mean little if they're not followed by movement. Action becomes the bridge between insight and embodiment. It is progress in motion.

Taking meaningful action is about doing what matters. What is aligned. What is alive. What is true. Think of action like planting a seed; you prepare the soil, water it with attention, and trust that something will grow. Or like building a bridge, one board at a time, toward a life that feels more whole.

When we take a Coach Approach, we don't push for action for action's sake. We invite it. We co-create it. We hold space for people to move at the speed of their own readiness, while staying connected to their deepest commitments. And progress doesn't always look like giant leaps. It often looks like one small step taken with clarity and courage, repeatedly. Not all action is loud or fast. Sometimes, it's a pause. A breath. A gentle but firm yes. Other times, it's a clear no. A boundary. A beginning.

The questions below are here to help you move from intention into motion from what you know to what you do.

- What's one small step you can take today that would move you forward?

- What action would nourish you, not just the goal?

- What would feel satisfying to complete this week?

- What boundary could you honor that would shift this dynamic?

- What's holding you back from taking this next step?

- What daily action would bring this vision closer?

- What's your level of commitment to seeing this through?

- What potential detours might arise and how might you meet them?

- What space will you give this on your calendar in the coming days?

- How will you recognize that you're moving in the right direction?

- What single step could launch this project with clarity?

- What will it take to bring this into being?

MONEY MATTERS: WHAT'S THE STORY YOU'RE LIVING

Money is more than numbers in an account, it's a mirror, a teacher, a current of energy shaped by beliefs, stories, and emotion. For some, money is a loaded word, wrapped in layers of fear, scarcity, guilt, or silence. For others, it's a neutral instrument, a simple exchange of value.

Like a river, money flows most freely where channels are clear and banks are sturdy. It can carve through resistance or pool in unexpected places. How we relate to money often reveals how we relate to receiving, deserving, trusting, and creating. Is your relationship with money one of struggle, avoidance, gratitude or partnership?

Exploring this landscape with curiosity can illuminate where your financial flow may be blocked or flourishing. The goal is not just to "have more," but to cultivate a conscious and empowered money philosophy, one that aligns with your values, supports your needs, and reflects your sense of enoughness.

Whether you see money as a trusted ally or an uncomfortable mystery, the questions below are designed to help you become more aware, more grounded, and more choiceful about how money moves through your life.

- What does money mean to you, not just practically, but emotionally?

- How have your earliest memories about money shaped your current beliefs?

- How would having more money change the way you live, give, or create?

- What leads you to believe that earning money must be hard work?

- How much is "enough" for you?

- Who influenced your money story, and which parts of that story still feel true?

- What's the truth about your current relationship with money if you let yourself be completely honest?

- When are you most likely to spend impulsively, and what need might that be trying to meet?

- What systems or habits help you feel more empowered and grounded in your finances?

- How comfortable are you with the flow of money in and out of your life each month?

- What does "financial well-being" mean for you, not just in numbers, but in how it feels?

- If money were a river, what might be blocking the flow and what would it take to open it again?

HOW ARE YOU CONNECTED?

Human beings are wired for connection. Like trees in a forest whose roots intertwine beneath the surface, we are sustained by the relationships that hold us, seen and unseen. We are always in community of some kind: with ourselves, with others, with nature, with ideas, with animals, with ancestors, and even with silence. Community is not just the people gathered around us. It's the field of belonging that nourishes our becoming.

Yet not all communities are chosen consciously. Sometimes, we wake up and realize we've been living within systems or circles that no longer align with who we are. Other times, we find ourselves yearning for deeper resonance for people and places that meet us in truth and joy.

Part of the journey of self-leadership is choosing and tending the communities that matter most whether it's a circle of trusted friends, a creative partnership, a spiritual fellowship, or simply one kindred spirit who sees you clearly.

Community can uplift or deplete. It can mirror back your light or dull your voice. The invitation is to reflect: What kinds of communities nourish you? And what kind do you want to cultivate going forward?

Sometimes, just one heartfelt connection can shift everything.

Here are some questions to help you reflect on your communities and relationships:

- Who is your greatest advocate and how do they impact your life?

- What kind of people do you choose to surround yourself with?

- What community, if any, do you find yourself yearning for?

- Which of your current communities nourish you most deeply?

- What, if anything, would you change about your circle of friends?

- What kind of relationship do you have with your neighbors or local circle?

- How often do you connect meaningfully with those you care about?

- What traditions or rituals help you feel rooted in your family or chosen community?

- In what ways do you contribute to your family, spiritual, or social communities?

- How does engaging in any service, volunteerism, or mutual aid feed you?

- What group brings out your joy, play, or creativity?

- What would your ideal, soul-aligned community feel like?

THE WORK
YOU'RE HERE TO DO

Just like in life, it's important to regularly check in on your career or business and ensure it aligns with what truly matters to you. After all, much like tending a garden, your career or business requires ongoing care, pruning, and attention. It's easy to fall into routine, to show up, do the work, and move on, without stopping to ask whether what you're doing still nourishes your spirit. Yet, given how much of your life is devoted to making a living, it's vital that this aspect of your life is not just sustainable, but meaningful.

When your work aligns with your core values and allows space for your unique gifts to flourish, it becomes more than just a way to earn a paycheck. It becomes a reflection of who you are and what you stand for. In this way, your work becomes part of your life's legacy.

Whether you're an entrepreneur building something from the soil up, or working within a larger organization, checking in regularly can help ensure you're growing in the direction of your truth. Is your current path helping you become who you want to be? Are you in integrity with what matters most?

Work, like life, shifts with the seasons. What once fit may now feel too small. Or perhaps there's an unexplored passion quietly calling from the edges. The questions below are offered as signposts to help you explore and reconnect with the purpose, vitality, and values that you bring to your professional life.

- What fulfills you in your career or business?

- What part of your job do you enjoy the most?

- What would make your work feel more fulfilling?

- How does your work contribute to your life goals?

- What is your vision for your career or business?

- Who in your work life brings out the best in you?

- What energizes you about your work?

- What is your biggest challenge in the workplace?

- What would change your attitude about your job?

- What aspects of your workplace can you actually control?

- How can you add more value to your clients, customers, or colleagues?

- What part of your career happened by chance?

THE HEART OF HOW YOU RELATE

Relationships are the mirror and the fire, the dance and the stillness. They are how we learn to be both seen and unseen, how we practice giving and receiving, and how we discover our own edges and softness. Whether romantic, familial, collegial, or platonic relationships shape our inner world and give texture to our outer life.

Some say we are not born into the world, but into relationship, into a web of connections that continue to grow and shift throughout our lives. The people we walk beside can reflect our deepest truths and our hidden fears. They can challenge our assumptions, inspire our evolution, and call us home to ourselves.

Strong, nourishing relationships are not simply the result of luck. They require attention, boundaries, curiosity, repair, and courage. And even the strained or complex ones offer rich soil for insight, growth, and learning.

You are always in relationship with others, yes, but also with yourself, your past, your future, your environment, your time, your truth. Exploring how you relate is a path of self-discovery.

Here are some questions to help you reflect on your relationships:

- What relationships feel most nourishing to you right now?

- Who helps you feel seen, safe, and supported?

- What patterns do you notice in your closest relationships?

- What stories are you carrying about relationships that no longer serve you?

- What boundaries would serve you better?

- Where in your relationships are you not speaking your truth?

- What does "healthy relationship" mean to you?

- Who challenges you in a way that helps you grow?

- Where are you giving more than feels sustainable?

- What relationships feel like obligation rather than choice?

- How do you tend to repair when there's been a rupture?

- What part of you gets revealed most often in relationships?

THE POWER AND PRESENCE OF CHOICE

At every turn, we are choosing, consciously or not. Choice is the quiet brushstroke painting the canvas of our lives. Even when the path seems carved by someone else's hand, our response is still ours to shape. We may not always choose the circumstances we face, but we do choose how we stand within them. That, too, is power.

Each decision is like a steppingstone laid across a river. Some feel stable, others wobble but all move us forward in some way. And if the stone you chose doesn't lead where you'd hoped? Step again. Realign. Choose anew. Life, thankfully, offers us endless invitations to pivot, recommit, or begin again. This section is not about "getting it right", it's about becoming more aware of how your choices shape the rhythm and flow of your life.

Here are some questions to help you explore your relationship with choices and decisions:

- Where in your life do you feel like you have no choice?

- What do you believe about having a choice?

- What if you could change the situation?

- What happens when you feel overwhelmed by choices?

- What is one decision you can make right now to get things moving?

- What choice could you make that would make you feel freer and lighter?

- What is the gift in the choice you've made?

- What feels scary about this decision?

- What would be different for you if you made this choice?

- What part of your life is by design?

- How do you expand what you believe is possible?

BEFORE WE CLOSE

As we near the end of this little guide of questions and reflections, it feels essential to pause, not only in silence, but in gratitude.

No journey of insight or contribution is ever ours alone. We are shaped, stretched, and supported by those who walk beside us, those who came before, and those who call us into becoming.

You may also be curious to explore some of those that have influenced and offer further perspectives that deepen your relationship with the art of questioning. Below is a thoughtfully curated selection of books that support personal growth, coaching mastery, leadership development, and the transformational power of inquiry. Whether you're seeking poetic insight, practical frameworks, or new ways of being in conversation, these texts offer inspiration, tools, and perspective. Enjoy!!

Adams, Marilee. (2004) Change Your Questions, Change Your Life. Berrett-Koehler. A foundational guide to shifting from judgment to learning by transforming the way we ask questions.

Particularly helpful for coaches and leaders navigating limiting mindsets.

Berger, Warren. (2014) A More Beautiful Question: The Power of Inquiry to Spark Breakthrough Ideas. Bloomsbury. An engaging look at how "why," "what if," and "how" questions fuel creativity, innovation, and possibility at work and in life.

Berger, Warren. (2018) The Book of Beautiful Questions. Bloomsbury. A practical follow-up with hundreds of curated questions designed to improve decision-making, creativity, relationships, and leadership communication.

Bohns, Vanessa. (2021) You Have More Influence Than You Think. W. W. Norton & Company. Explores how subtle cues—like questions—carry weight in our daily lives. A psychology-based exploration of relational influence and unseen impact

Brown, Brené. (2021) Atlas of the Heart: Mapping Meaningful Connection and the Language of Human Experience. Random House. An illuminating reference on human emotion, packed with language and inquiry to explore inner and relational worlds with precision and care.

Csikszentmihalyi, Mihaly. (1990) Flow: The Psychology of Optimal Experience. Harper & Row. A classic that explores how attention, curiosity, and presence create meaningful, engaging lives—offering insight into how we might shape our questions to foster "flow."

Elder, Linda & Paul, Richard. (2006) The Miniature Guide to the Art of Asking Essential Questions. Foundation for Critical Thinking. A concise and accessible guide that explores how to frame questions for clarity, reasoning, and critical thinking—perfect for educational and professional settings.

Goldberg, Marilee. (1998) The Art of the Question. John Wiley & Sons, Inc. A pioneering book on how powerful questions shape our thoughts, decisions, and possibilities. A classic in the coaching field.

Gregersen, Hal. (2018) Questions Are the Answer: A Breakthrough Approach to Your Most Vexing Problems at Work and in Life. Harper Business. A research-based guide to cultivating "catalytic questioning" in leadership and innovation, full of tools to shift the quality of inquiry.

Palmer, Parker J. (2004) A Hidden Wholeness: The Journey Toward an Undivided Life. Jossey-Bass. An invitation into courageous self-reflection and dialogue. Palmer offers a contemplative lens on presence and integrity in relationships—with self and others.

Parker, Priya. (2018). The Art of Gathering: How We Meet and Why It Matters. Riverhead Books. Not about questions directly—but about intentional design of space and connection. A valuable resource for facilitators, group coaches, and anyone creating containers for transformation.

Schein, Edgar. (2021) Humble Inquiry, 2nd Edition: The Gentle Art of Asking Instead of Telling. Berrett-Koehler. A coaching-aligned approach to leading with curiosity and humility. Offers powerful principles for asking in a way that invites openness and trust.

Stock, Gregory. (2013) The Book of Questions: Revised and Updated. Workman Publishing. A beloved classic—hundreds of provocative, ethical, playful, and profound questions designed to spark self-reflection and conversation.

Tippett, Krista. (2016) Becoming Wise: An Inquiry into the Mystery and Art of Living. Penguin Press. Drawn from interviews on her On Being podcast, this book weaves soulful inquiry into topics like love, beauty, language, and resilience.

Whyte, David. (2019 reissue; originally 2001) Consolations: The Solace, Nourishment and Underlying Meaning of Everyday Words. Many Rivers Press. Poetic essays on ordinary words like "Courage," "Regret," "Friendship," and "Genius," each framed as a meditation and a kind of question unto itself.

ACKNOWLEDGMENTS

This guide is rooted in decades of practice, presence, and learning. I offer deep gratitude to all those who have shaped my path, not only as a professional coach, but more importantly, as a human being in evolution.

To my teachers, colleagues, mentors, and clients: thank you for challenging me, inspiring me, and reminding me—over and over again—what it means to meet each moment with compassion, curiosity, and wholehearted presence.

And to my family, my first and most enduring circle of love. To Mick Whelan, my life partner (and "hubby" in the truest, most devoted sense), thank you for your unwavering patience, humor, and support. To my amazing children, who continue to teach me about joy, resilience, and what matters most, thank you for being exactly who you are. I wouldn't be who I am without you.

With love and profound appreciation to all who walk this journey with me.

This concludes the Mini Pocket Guide: Curious Coaching Questions.

May these questions serve not as a script, but as inspiration, inviting you to trust your intuition, expand your presence, and deepen your impact. Use them as companions on your journey, both personally and professionally, and remember: the best questions are the ones that arise from presence, curiosity, and care.

ABOUT THE AUTHOR
PAMELA RICHARDE

A devoted explorer of inner and outer worlds, Pamela Richarde, MA, MCC brings an eclectic blend of wisdom, rigor, and wonder to all she does. With a background that spans multiple disciplines, cultures, and ways of knowing, her insatiable curiosity has led her into lifelong inquiry across scientific and spiritual realms alike.

For over 30 years, Pamela has devoted her work to coaching. A pioneer in the profession, she is a Master Certified Coach, trainer, mentor, and passionate advocate for coaching excellence. She is a founding member of the International Coaching Federation (ICF), where she also served as Global President and Vice Chair of the ICF Coaching Education Board.

Pamela holds a BA in Political Science and an MA in Acting, is a 2nd Degree Black Belt in ShaoLin Kung Fu, and is a longtime practitioner of Tai Chi Chuan. Through her company, InnerVision Enterprises, she continues to serve individuals and organizations worldwide offering pathways to insight, presence, and transformative change.

Contact: Info@InnerVisionEnterprises.com